These Hollowed Bones

Books by Amelia Díaz Ettinger

Self Dissection

Learning to Love a Western Sky

Fossils On A Red Flag

Speaking at a Time: Hablando a la Vez

These Hollowed Bones
Poems

Published 2024 by Sea Crow Press
Barnstable, MA
www.seacrowpress.com

Paperback ISBN: 978-1-961864-00-9
Ebook ISBN: 978-1-961864-01-6
Library of Congress Control Number: 2023941122

Cover Image by Dale Chaplin
Cover Design by Mary Petiet
Interior Design by Mary Petiet

Praise for Amelia Díaz Ettinger

These Hollowed Bones is, fittingly, flighted on hope and feathers. Díaz Ettinger flawlessly bridges the perceived divide between us and our winged brethren to uncover worlds of shared intimacy—both within our shared world and ourselves. We have always looked to the sky for answers, found our dreams of flight the most wondrous. In this collection, such wonderment unfolds effortlessly on the page with the poet's sprawling knowledge dovetailed perfectly with an artist's eye.

— Jessica Mehta, author of *Constellations of My Body*

In *These Hollowed Bones* Ettinger acts as an ornithologist drawing on her astute observations of birds to convey her message. Throughout the collection it is these sharp images and motifs that create an atmosphere of longing whether for a deeper closeness to her mother or an exploration of her heritage. It is Ettinger's encounters with birds that reflect some of our most vulnerable human qualities.

— TAK Erzinger, poet, winner of the 2021 Whirling Prize, University of Indianapolis

Within the pages of *These Hollowed Bones* Amelia Díaz Ettinger has assembled a flock of poems that sing complex and haunting songs of ancestry, migration, ageing, and loss. Set against the backdrop of a world reshaped by climate change and fire, Ettinger's birds bank between metaphor and persona, sometimes standing in for family members and sometimes inhabited by the poet herself. But whether perched in the loneliness of an empty nest or yearning for her home country, like the birds she writes about, Ettinger knows "that fear flees when there's community". Ettinger's poems build that community, that "gifted grace of a murmuration," through the precise and tender lens of an ornithologist's eye, a poet's eye. *These Hollowed Bones* is a brilliant "theater of synchronicity," a collection the reader can come home to again and again, in any season.

— Brittany Corrigan, author of *Solastalgia*

These Hollowed Bones

POEMS

Amelia Diaz Ettinger

Sea Crow Press

For my mother Emilia Barrios Ruiz, it was a privilege to finally meet you, even if it was for such a short time.

Tu hija por siempre—

Contents

Iguaca xii

Cotorrita Puertoriqueña
Amazona vittata

cotorrita, cotorrita de la frente colorá
son tus ojos los espejos
de la vida que se va

Puerto Rican Parrot
Amazona vittata

little parrot, little parrot
forehead so bright
your eyes mirror
the extinguishing life

i

Towhee

Pipilo erythrophthalamus

for no particular reason
on these walks of mine
my bird is the Towhee
—Rufous-Sided to be exact
i like her unassuming
dress of brown
with hints of white patches
flashing on her tail
as she flies towards a branch
but maybe what calls
me to her is her song
chup chup chup seeeeeeeeee
such a plain song
a clear song
a celebration song
makes me wonder
how can she be so content
in her noisy rummage
among dead leaves
that startles me awake?
such a necessary reminder
to sing

Brewer's or Grackle

Euphagus cyanocephalus or
Quiscalus niger?

i'm always home, but wistfulness follows
me as tail feathers on a bird—a Brewer's blackbird
they cluster on the wooden broken fence
near our reeds—males with their curious yellow eyes

that seems to shift lost crevices inside of me,
their iridescent heads—that purple shimmer
an oil stain green, these lushness takes me back
to a childhood of tropical rain, Fichus trees,

and a plaza filled with the *chinchilín* song
of his cousin—an ecological equivalent—
the Antillean Grackle
could i beg for a similar fortune?

if my wish were granted, the child in me would run
unabashed after that long tailed chango
the perfect name for a silly bird that shows off
his large family—a gatherer full of mischief,

but the Grackle is not here in this colder climate
here the aloof Brewer's, secretive but for singing
his own cacophonous song to his immediate brood
i can sense he doesn't feel the loss of home

unlike me, his home is home—where the nest rests
its twiggy cup near brothers and sisters
a loose colony of familiar ancestry—my jealousy
at least for this summer, for this breeding season

Brown-headed Cowbird
Molothrus ater

I know what it's said about me
that I am a bad mother
a brood parasite
—no
I know I relinquish
my eggs to the care of others
but notice; I take my time
watching in torture-wait until
I find her,
the perfect host
a serious, smaller, caring
female in this fragile world
where hatchlings are unattended
—no

even though you think I'm vile
to throw one —or two—of her
eggs out of her nest,
my babies will hatch first
it's not my fault
she prefers their size
and look—
who can resist their opened
beaks, a rosy-red
that disgraces any flower
—no

I do what I naturally do
to make sure my own
have the best success
you can call me what you may
—but in my place,
for the sake of them
—not your own
would you
have the courage
to do the same?

The Wild Turkey Is a Good Mother

Meleagris gallopavo

a native to the Americas
with a name derived by accident,
what did they know in England?

when you arrived at those shores
from boats ferried by Turkish merchants
i prefer your name in Spanish—Gallopavo

kin to the Gallinules that walk on water
lilies that dress in raucous colors—not you
—except for your head, you are dowdy

better for concealment as you lay
your eggs on dry leaves, and land
unsteady—and loud—on tree branches

you're boisterous without melody, but the reward
in the camaraderie of your rafters
aunts, mothers, and grandmothers take care

of everyone's poult as their own
—that is why you thrive while the male
opens his wings and tail to allure—

and i wonder how it is to receive all that sheen
from love, from care?

Black-capped Chickadee

Poecile atricapilla

its daintiness is deceiving
with looks so frail, and yet

they suffer winter storms
in these brutal mountains—a banditry

after a blizzard, they speckle
the blinding snow with *dee-dee-dee*

a song reminiscent of spring
in the death of frost

maybe that is why I think of her—Emilia
when i see these tiny nearly tame acrobats

foraging in naked branches finding
morsels where i see none

—perhaps

i was late to meet her, her warmth
the way she blanketed

my shoulders in a hug
how she gave me tidbits for decades lost

in this tiny bird's industrious energy, i see
her paused steps among the Mexican streets

she shared with the family she nurtured
as formidable as a chickadee
—my mother

Crested Caracara
Caracara cheriway

i have never seen a Crested Caracara,
and this doubles my losses

the Mexican Eagle
—she is a falcón

that runs with vultures
and builds nests of sticks

nobility of feathers
that weave the history

of la raza—she tells
stories from cradle

—to coffin

she gave the seed of maíz
to the people, and once
she flew to the sun

that's why her beak turned gold
while she carried a scissortail
on her back to safety
her legs grew long

clutching the nopal
with a serpent in her talons
the clear and assured sign
to the Mexica, her chosen place
to build Tenochtitlán

how i wish i had grown
with her voice

—my flight from her shores
my shortfall

Guavate (Carite) Forest with Tody, 1969

Todus mexicanus

i stood on the edge,
and screamed,
i was seventeen

in this forest, Guavate,
where I often found peace,
even in the company of papi

my outburst scurried lizards
over crunched leaves

but the frogs went silent,
—quiescent censorship

to my anger

a San Pedrito landed
on a vibrating,
insubstantial branch.

green, pink, and slight
with an orange beak
looking like a baton of disdain

his black pupil expanded
as our eyes met
—his fear subsided

his gifted presence
my shame as he flew away

Fly South Like an Arctic Tern!

Sterna paradisaea

i say to myself, mostly in jest, when my tide is low
but even standing on this lava rock from an eroding volcano

long extinct on this Oregon coast, i can't see far enough
not near enough

i stand protected from freeways, motorcars, and wings—
things that travel fast could take me to turn a life for another

but this ocean cold-gray, indifferent
i know—i listen—to its waves and feel its foamy spray

an arctic tern just flew over—black feathers paste a cap
sleek like a tango dancer's pomade, she is a *bailarina*

is she pointing the way for me? is she my oracle to travel?
Kee yah she screeches *winter hides behind these clouds*

her translucent wings so delicate to make her monumental
journey
and still she is not daunted—she can choose her fate

she doesn't wonder what axis of this planet belongs to her
at ease with her luck in life she flies to her destination

maybe i should follow her and learn myself in another coast,
maybe i will get used to the cry of a bandoneón

and learn to dance

ii

Tyrannidae

Empidonax traillii

i hesitate to mention the flycatchers
just saying that name out loud—*fly catcher*

conjures untold dreams—*dreams*
caught in gossamer fibers of imagination

and yet, for me, they reminded of a time
when i ran curious—untethered, sallied forth

to snap insects in midair
from any branch we chose

with legs as swift as feathers
then anything was possible

when i was a bird
and my colors

were their colors
and we could carol an undeveloped

song
even
when i
banded
you
in a nest
to wait
a
future
now
bygone
to remind me of my youth —

no wonder you're called—
the tyrant

Red-tailed Hawk

Buteo jamaicencis

You are a common dweller under this sky
right here next to Mount Harris
along these plowed fields of grass

are you ever confused
with your Jamaican moniker?
after all,

deer mice found fecund in these fields
see you perching
on electric poles designed for your wingspan

so easily christened by that redness
flashing proud through your tail feathers
like a flare of sun

appointed after an island deep in the Caribbean
yet you are here—while i despair
not a Mexican, or a Carib,

not a native Oregonian
i wish to be a vole you chase
to care only about the safety
of shadc

Bufflehead
Bucephala albeola

for S. M. and so many others Earth's lovers

a birder died today, his bird
was the bufflehead

he pursued with camera at heart,
delightful record of dives, his certain aim

a Goldeneye with the fisheye lens
frame by frame netting

the vanishes of graceful magic, reappearance
in the soft ripples of double image

how could he not be riveted
by the small dancer of the sea?

a large head with enviable feathers
buoyant and alert, just like the man

who kept vigilance of dance
of song, of graceful life

WINTER BIRD

Ave testimonia

You have seen the leaves of autumn drop
—so, you know how my love has been
not in the tumble, but the branches

which turn their naked fingers to catch
your weight with the frost that is sure to come
the vulnerability of it makes me shudder

i see the cold in how you fluff your body
how you turn you gaze towards me
our landscapes going light and fruitless

You and i can go back
to another season, another turn
— why does it have to hurt?

You know it does—
You are the witness
to fall—to winters

Least Sandpiper

Erolia minutilla

For my granddaughter

Your name is so pleasant—*minutilla*
wish i'd thought of you
when *Andie* was born

a little speckle of a girl
like you—a *peeps*
not much bigger than a sparrow

with challenges of her own
will she be brave, like you,
and roam the arctic in summer

then follow a rhythm to Brazil?
will she discover
the pleasures of mudflats

grassy marshes
and seek dragonflies?
will she sing

a lyrical *kree-eet*
to a coterie of birds
especially here, with me

under this Western sky?

—This shorebird migrates thousands of miles between

its arctic breeding grounds then winters
as far south as Chile and Brazil.

The Dark Blue of a Steller's Jay

Cyanocitta stelleri

i hide behind bushes like a cat, pounce or screech to scare it
—and eternally fail in my skirmishes
with this Steller's Jay

once, i threw a rake while he squawked and grumbled
what is with this bird? makes noise at all hours of the day
especially at dawn, when i rather languish in the comfort of
warm sheets

it is a steadfast vision at my birdfeeder, meant for birds with
lyrical tunes,
not those unsettling raucous notes, so inharmonious
i even put suet in a cage within a cage—it didn't sway

go, find yourself another home! he still manages to steal the
sweetness.

today was the first snow of this year, and the birdfeeder was full
of seeds
my husband plans ahead, for the tiny birds i love—those brave
enough, don't fly south
he remembers their care before i do—he need to prepare for a
hard winter

*help you bring those song birds you love so much—time to let the
corvids go*

he is right

time to shave my head, he adds in a casual voice
birdseeds cling to his flannel coat along full loads of his white
hair,
snatched too soon by chemo.

i'm always last to think—the clippers buzz and i'm careful not
to let a single strand
fall
on the ground
his lovely locks are toxic—they can't line the nests next spring

that is sure to come, regardless of my hesitation
his shorn scalp blends translucent against the fallen snow
a light kiss on it feels foreign

i clutch his hair in my hand—not ready to let it go
he turns sudden to add, *look!*
it is that Cyanocitta that has robbed our morning's sleep these
many years

the blue was so swift, it surprised us both
what do you call that kind of blue? it's beautiful
cyanno means dark blue, the color of loss—i can't answer
we watch in wonder as the Jay flutters and i clench
the hand that still holds his hair
you should wear that color, he smiles and rubs his new
bald head

a compliment to thank me for this deed, this dread

how strange silence grows around us
the Steller's sits on a leafless branch of our hawthorn—early
winter

the branch bounces slightly at the loss of his weight

now, i wish he could stay here forever singing off key

Western Bluebird

Siália mexicána

in the morning,

the Bluebird carried a fecal sack
far away from her nest
a tidy demonstration of care and order

while that evening

my lover discharged his gun inside our home
five deafening bullets—each shot a mark
for a life he finds floundering its purpose

his anger a cocktail of disease and vodka
on a rare night of respite from summer's
heat and fire smoke

this spring,

the Sialia chose tenderness, i've witnessed her losses
—her first and second clutch erased her possibilities
the first to this climate heat that seared her chicks

then to the predator who destroyed her careful nest
such common savagery is nature's way, i guess—
now she tends this new brood heartedly, but i wonder

does she also carry
the desolate shards
of empty bullets?

Mystical Woodpecker

Talthybius malomen

my binoculars are covered in pollen
—so it must be summer at last
and here comes that Woodpecker,
the mystical one,
the one i invented, for times like these

his feathers are made of steel
his beak is neither gold nor hope
pure bone on flesh
brings a sort of peace
in heat, dust, and sorrow

i saw him again today
when with trembling hands
i raised my ringing phone,
that hideous Talthybius,
i could not answer

i no longer listen
let time rip my bones apart
for now,
i'd rather watch my imaginary bird
through yellowed lenses

The Preternatural Bird

Ignominious imagination

if only i believed in an afterlife
—i would reincarnate
with barbs, wings, and talons
that steal flies from a pine cone deep
in these woods—to uncover shelter in midair
or in the bark of a luscious tamarack with its blood interior

if i were this bird, i would percussion my beak until i got inside
the cambium of any tree or tin roof—just to wake the living
with a crescendo of hammerlike hullabaloos until they squeal—
we want to sleep—in that cry, i would laugh away, garbling
a song
of joy with these long wings and tatter feathers.

and exit in fight-display
two streamers of long bright plumes—noble enough to be a scis-
sor-tail
and i would tease your breath away
just to see you squirm and wish
you could be me

—if only

iii

Ruddy Duck

Oxyura jamaicensis

maybe it is all in how i see you
a bit of a clown
absurd webbed-blue feet
on legs set too far back
—helpless on land

maybe it is your spiky tail
so high, so self-assured
on a chunky circus body
black, white, and iron-rust
yes, that might be—

then, perhaps it is in your silence
except when you're in lust
bubbling the water with percussion
from air sacks secreted

whatever it is you are
the marsh comedian
whom i turn in pain
to make me smile

Black-headed Grosbeaks

Pheucticus melanocephalus

to my surprise as i wonder
about this morning's nature gift,
in Roger Tory Peterson's field guide
the towhee and the grosbeaks
live side by side, frozen in profile

Grosbeaks seldom visit us
here in these dense fir and larch woods
sunshine reaches slowly as the sun
toils through branches and opens
in the meadow to our south

my myopic eyes awoke to the sight
of a gross of males and a female
swirling in the frenzy of spring desire
right here on this lawn, this privilege
i became a voguer in an avian drama

a spread of feathers and silent competition
the female feeds on bits left over
by the lawnmower—pretending
she does not see the wings spread
for her delight, her rhapsody

ahh, to be that young again

Pileated Woodpecker

Dryocopus pileatus

most likely a mating dance
or just 'stay with me for this season'

to witness is a gift,
a dance up and down a grand fir

turned maypole for this dramatic duo
red crest aflame and uncommonly quiet

nothing of their raucous *kik — kikkik*
no drumming on bark to wake this forest

no—a silent dance of black and red feathers up
and down prehensile tails make it possible

to stand with frozen wingbeats
longing stares white underwings

adverted from everyone else's vision
just each other exist in this private ritual

what is it like to move so freely in the open,
pirouetting in fevered sunshine?

what is it like to keep view of your lover,
even if it's only for one more summer?

Mourning Dove

Zenáida macroúra

the avian rascal of the Columbiformes
a total misnomer of the name—mourning
you remind me of high school girls

the ones at recess
wanting to find
a boy to flirt

they used to sing a doleful sound
to gain attention, *Oh, Oh, Oh!*
—a certain snare

listen—

what is there to lament?
you can drink salt in water
to your crop's content

populate the continent
from shore to shore
suburbs to heartland

—and there is your flight,
swift and direct
there is no glide or gile

hear—

how you tease
following your mate
with another suitor at your side

do you engage in a menage à trois?
when you sing *ooah-ooo-oo-o*
is it gloom or impish song?

i have so much to learn

Wilson's Phalarope

Steganopus tricolor

i relish watching
you at Ladd March

—Oregon's hidden oasis
of ducks and shorebirds—

gaudily dressed in mating
extravagant female plumage

you wear the tricolors
in your house

what a delight it's to see your needle
beak as it harpoons the water

as you swim in those tight circles
—some may even think you're mad

but the vortex you create
brings prey to the surface

and of course, your polyandry
is not anti-patriarchy

you are unaware of our biases
and i admit to admire

—that you leave your eggs
for your mates to tidy up and care

are you aware how inspirational you are?

Western Gull

Larus occidentalis

you've been called,

—an opportune feeder
of saltwater and flotsam

with a yellow beak stained
red like a beauty mark

—mischievous, stealing milk
from a sleeping mother seal

— gregarious, flocking along
same-minded birds to steal
their hard-earned morsels

—versatile as you walk the sands and
rocky shores and, of course, a forager
that delights in untethered heights

—and yet you're a beachcomber
seldom seen inland
your passion is the shore
where you mate

sometimes with another female
you lay your eggs together with her
season after breeding season

no one to tell you—scandalous
and how you made scientist scramble
to find a name, a reason, a forced excuse
for your nature,

let me call you
—trailblazer

Pygmy Owl

Glaucidium gnoma

i saw a clump of leaves
oddly unmoving on a naked
branch
small
tight
curiously symmetrical
then it moved

her head
—a small Shirobheda movement
like an Indie dancer
on a body
no bigger than my fist
astonished to see
her double face
—the goddess
Shakti?—

the feathers on her back
making mock-eyes
and i—the *Homo sapiens*
fell for this fauna hoax
—but chickadees and sparrows
are no dupes

"there she is!"
they mobbed and shrieked
"the villain!"
"I saw her catch a starling"
"she robbed a robin's nest"
"and flew to rancher's barn
caught a chicken ten times
her size."

her true yellow
round disks of light
found mine
i startled,

"Are these stories true?" i asked her.

"Are you surprised?" the bundle of leaves replied
"It's my nature as a small female I know
what to take"

Black-chinned Hummingbird
Archilochus alexandri

you take your name from the male,
don't fret, it's not your fault, it's ours

we glory at his colors and yet
you're who comes every day to feast

on the insects that fly over still water
late in the day when others are at roost

quiet but by the wind whorl of your wings
that steer a sound akin to heart beats

i often wonder if you delight in your image—an avian narcissus
over our pond? you should, that double reflection in water

two birds for one—i bet you don't demur
being a bit drabber—no black and violet chin

as it stands you can be confused
with the Costas or Ruby-throated

good! let them wonder as you shine, grow
and astonish, you deserve your splendor

—incognita

Lazuli Bunting Song

Passerina amoena

small beautiful bird,
what can you teach me?

undoubtedly, you light up a drab day
with a flash of turquoise and rust in an ordinary

thicket—your jumbled melody—a macho seduction
to keep territory and secure that soft

colored female—impossible not to notice
your brilliant lapis— not unsimilar

to men in suits who hold sway,
you do it without chicanery, you take

notice one chick, one brood, one
neighborly ballad at a time

—as a yearling you learned your neighbor's solo
collective notes scattered around the hamlet to keep peace

among rivals that want the same
you reach harmony while you listen

small beautiful bird,
what can you teach me?

House Wren

Troglodytes aedon

to have so much in common with a brown bird
especially now during this pandemic

she and i cave dwellers—troglodytes that gnaw
at seeds, insects, and time—she awaits her brood

to grow and fly away—while i long for my children
to return to this garden to play and forage

we bide our lives in this same meadow
she a gifted songster that gurgles and stutters

while my voice rises in bursts of silent loneliness
we let each other share this side-by-side communion

her black eye eyes my own as i near her wooden house
over the fence of my garden—her tail-cocks a wave

i say hello with two fingers at my temple
—the grace between neighbors

as i nibble an apricot—she feasts on a moth
we dream of company soon

Western Meadowlark

Sturnella neglecta

no one does springtime like you
stocky brown with white banners

reminiscent of surrender flags
a ceasefire of your own

though lewis and clark
forgot to mention you, so your name

'neglecta' among Blackbirds and Orioles,
but abandoned you are not

you have the sheen—fêted to be Oregon's bird
like those pursuers, the pioneers

—you look for open wide spaces
grassland to conquer without a pilfer

spring livens with your melodic
watery call, nature's flute

you perch on demarcating fences
puffing your yellow chest

to proudly display your black 'V'
as if etched by a child's marker

what do you say as you sing
your double notes?

you are right
to show this pride

Familiarity Breeds Invisibility

Junco oreganus

not to rob the Tanager's orange and yellow surprise
after all, she brings the happiness of a ripe apple in June—

nor to steal the gusto of Warblers—
yellow, green, darts about a bush with gabbled song

or the marvel of a Condor's wide span, which carries the
whole sky
with the mastery of all birds of prey—

binoculars seldom span for the ubiquitous junco,
it's just a junco—i've heard often enough

but consider the Junco's small brown body,
her darkest eyes—our own familiarity

with her panic flights full of toil, her loose musical trill—
outer tail feathers two long white banners

in the deep of winter in this Oregon town, she
keeps company in the quiet of a snow storm

in that white death—she's who moves our landscape—
brings a bit of warmth with her relentless foraging in bare
branches

in this endless frozen sea,
she is our familiar surprise —

—Passeriformes
Migrate Freely in February

feathered clouds swirl,
billow over the edge
of freeways

mixed flocks,
Robins, Snow Buntings
the Songbirds flying together as one

over an ocean of snow
—the remains of a belated blizzard
they cast blue shadows

they are a school of mixed birds,
lift and land on the verge,
—a mirage-ballet of risk

so close to moving traffic

their camaraderie is silent
morsels exposed on asphalt
found and shared

here a discarded bone,
a pebble, lost treasures
in late winter

for now, they are one wing, one eye
spring and mating will eventually bring
the inevitable segregation

their fate assured by the laws of nature
does human migration share this kind of joy?
this theater of synchronicity?

Clark's Nutcracker

Nucífraga columbiána

after the breeding season
we often find odd mates
like this Clark's Nutcracker and a Sterling Jay

sharing a morsel of bagels
in the parking lot of Anthony Lakes
they don't fight, they simply share

while a few children, without masks,
ride the see-saw built to make bikers out of them
their father watches with arms ready to catch

across from the birds another family unloads their toys
and the birds lift and flutter away simultaneous
watching intently with identical expressions

they must be famished—with their young gone
time to fatten for the winter that is yet to come
—a child drops a bag of chips, the birds

dive together to catch the booty— again, they stay close
it's the end of a summer hotter than usual with fire smoke
and exhaustion from isolation—but today the cerulean sky

has brought them out, the sun shines without a curtain
scavenging together makes me wonder if darwin
had it wrong, here i see a simple joy

—the Clark's beak tenderly picks
at a chip on the Steller's and both crackle
in a chaunt not far from laughter

iv

Sparrow Hawk and The Nester

Fálco sparvérius

I nearly reached the water
the longest and shortest
journey— even if I have a thousand
legs in all

mornings were full of dew
at first, I didn't perish,
so many died before
my brothers and sisters
did they climb the grasses
to take a drink?

the thirst in my pinchers
was deep, but I wondered
what a full swig of water
be? Would it be green
and taste of pollen?

thinking these water thoughts
pierced the worry of the Kestrel
—that Sparrow Hawk
flying so close by me day by day
I thought of those droplets
and imagined collecting each one
if I could burden the big water in me

the rest came in a mushroom
it was hollowed by age's decay
just a moment for a dream
of currents and rain and joy
the fullness of lichens
bathed in moisture
and tiny spiders that taste of glory

now my body waxes and wanes
others will get there first
so I settle to watch that kestrel
finally take her requite

Brown Pelican

Pelecánus occidentális

'A brown pelican was the first casualty,'

—Christina Zdanowicz

Oct 4 2021, CNN

I've never seen the ocean gray
—no, not gray— black
with a sheen that reflects
my flight, it blinds me
to the fish I know might be still
be low in its gruesome presence
the fish,
do they also swim in blindness?
I'm not alone in this hunger
we fly and fly in circles
the smell of salt is gone
the air tastes like metal boats
the boats,
I saw them flock
around this void
float in my Oceanhome
Oceanhome,
now it is a stranger to me
I coast low
to see
my feathers stick
with a coat
of this odd
black
liquid
mirr—

Songbirds

Aves coperativas

the Bootleg Fire leaves a canopy of gray
making it hard to breathe —or play

i brave the bad air outside to sit and sip
my coffee while i watch a bevy of birds

—seventeen species—in wonderment
by this pond hidden in the shadow of the Blues

Grossbeaks, Warblers, and Woodpeckers
taking turns to drink, bathe, and fortify each other

the Chipping Sparrow, Catbird, and Nuthatches
soak their wings to take water for their nest

i'm witnessing an avian cooperation in the heat
of this cruel summer, that had seared so many chicks

a second clutch—this hope—might succeed in a climate
that has gone awry—but for now i drink as they soak

contour feathers in the coolness of this tarn
hidden for the moment from fires—this Summerville water

that nurtures with the taste of fresh hope in this dread—
a bird's alarm echoes mine but as i hide in isolation

these birds know that fear flees when there's community
so, they've gathered here, a solidarity

to shelter away from this brutal heat and ashen air
by the fostering aspens and firs

—i seek their communion

Disappearing Bird, the Dipper

Cinclus mexicanus

we haven't met for a long while
where have you gone, my tiny friend?

your song half Mockingbird, part Wren
entertained the air with a mix

of rushing water and your *zeet*
aquatic song here in this climate-changing West

i recall your dip, disappearing—
camouflaged over steely boulders

and gray-crystal waters, preen and preen
your thick coat of feathers

at Wallowa River we visited
—me warming in the shade of an Aspen

as you flashed and blinked white eyelids
somnolent stretching each skinny leg

yawning, you made me yawn
your safety in this river secured

—or so we thought, even in the danger
of molting feathers late in summer

your slow disappearance
makes me wonder

A Gannet Named Nigel

Morus serrator

—The Washington Post by Karin Brulliard, February 6, 2018

should i be sad for Nigel
maybe bellow his loss?

he loved a cement
Gannet for all of his life

she was a decoy
a lure to bring more of his kind

and yet, for years he was faithful
he gave her fish and renovated their nest

she was everything to him season after season
his silent companion on an empty rocky shore

while her paint faded and no other gannets met
he waited by her side

for the sound of her and others
was his song different then in this void?

did he sing his throaty vibrato?
or did he wait to be far at sea to screech?

i don't know these things
but i know something about his seclusion

too afraid to venture far
now i live with decoys—images that talk inside of boxes

where i share a few fragments
in the safety of these flat screens

like Nigel—

i feed my solitude the best i can
try to find faith in a setting sun

while i cling to this hope—
a world full of Gannets and their full song

Double-crested Cormorant At Tamani Pesh-wa

Phalacrocorax auritus

driving down the gorge alongside the long ribbon of the Columbia
you see them pose "spread eagle"—witness prehistory

in the inky black of feathers that help them dive seeking crustaceans,
or small fish in those haughty beaks that they hold high

an aristocrat with the neck of a snake—easy figure
to identify in these waters which no longer hold wooden canoes

laden with fish to trade—*Auritus,* do you carry in your dense bones
how these waters rushed without the treachery of dams?

does the taste of Salmon, in these long-gone trading posts
marked with pictographs, linger on your tongue?

do you miss the aura of unrestrained water?
do you *see* the vigilance of *the One That Watches*?

Tsagaglalal guards your clever angle and silence
until you go to roost–your specter

is written on these rocks,
a keepsake

Ivory-billed Woodpecker
Campephilus principalis

could have been different
if I had the courage to raise
more chicks?

maybe gone north ?
or further west?
they didn't know me

as a dweller of sun
I wasn't a melancholic bird—

could I still taste a longhorn
larvae, delight in my gracious
flight?

we thought the trees
—those stately gods
would stay forever

there was a time,
that defies our memory,
we could fly for miles

without the sight of soil
that wonderful cover
of roots and joy

miles without gray lines
and the rush of metal
and exhaust

but the trees!
our trees
my trees,

they were so big and strong
If I preen my head against a bald cypress
bark, I think I can still hear pounding

our bills null the sounds of human drums
silenced by chainsaws
quieted all

our homes fell one
by one
leaving only roots like human fingers

attacking the air
or maybe imploring

yes, I should have kept moving north
or maybe west
had more chicks

but food was scarce
with *God-tree*'s leave
now, I'm the last

without a mate

my feathers
here
I lay to rest

Raven

Corvus corax

in 2020 the need for gatherings
was the surprise gift of a virus,

maybe it should have been palpable what matters
but then again, we lack foresight, just fear and aggravation

not able to do as one pleases—as if this planet was ours
—one day that year, i came across a murder within a murder

thousands of ravens on a Russian olive tree in the day's last heat
—silent vigil for the dead, she lay below in the shadow

from my narrow distance i could tell i had known her
this particular Corax without tail feathers

—this is what i remembered:

her loud vivacious *cr-r-ruck* in the morning by 'my' pond
across our shared meadow, she watched me as i gathered
vegetables

opportunistic neighbor! i delighted in her company,
this arial tumbler, her tender care and sly thievery

but that day within my isolation from the pestilence,

a logging truck swiped her while she gathered sticks for a nest
maybe hers' or her nieces'—she tumbled in the air landing

—inert

one by one the black gathering was the stillness in the tree
a devotion of sorrow feathers from up high

they sat perched wing against flank
heads holding wake, while the sunset turned to auburn

—i coveted her burial, those remembrances
under black feathers, that is what fastens

Magpies and Rubber Necks

Pica pica

a mischief of Magpies descends on a skunk carcass
by the side of the road

an odd frenzy
of black and white

they pick and pull
drunk from the discovery

tendons and hair split and torn
a few pecks at one another

a misshapen Magpie gets too close
the alpha notices and sends a trashing peck,

she hops a discolored retreat
masses arrive and surround the spectacle,

their hunger adverted by this voyeurism
like human traffic around an accident

the telephone lines fill

some Crows and Cowbirds have joined
the ruckus, a discordant cacophony,

for even here, news like these
this news, they travel fast

Sooty Tern

Sterna fuscata

the birds thought themselves safe
no barbwires in the open air

no red flags to shame their passage
they were safe, a home in the Caribbean,

a national wildlife refuge,
the first in the archipelago. [*1909*]

they came for the pleasure of white
and pink sands, and turquoise waters abundant

diving into those waters,
dropping like bombs from the sky,

you could hear their pleasure
in their straight narrow dives

Twin Rocks harbored their nests
this Caribbean Sea heralds the arrival

of the next generation
their jocular conglomerations

muted the sound of waves
a visible camaraderie

they were parents here, and aunts
and siblings

they knew and fed each other's chicks
—Safe—

a mighty small word
when all their white and black feathers darkened the sky

just seconds, while thousand
of Sooty Terns bathed

on a sea of rust
the inferno that followed

charred the anxious waiting families
sitting peacefully at their nests

Senator Goodel expressed concern, "the impact area an ecological disaster...the number that were destroyed is enormous."

Starlings in América

Sturnus vulgaris

The American Acclimation Society introduced the Starling in New York Central Park on March 6, 1890

look up at its feathers—the wonder
an astonishing purple iridescence,

chosen abode in América
for "*the enjoyment of Teutons and the Celtic race*"

the starling's beauty now unacknowledged
the dear bird a nuisance

the farmer down the road uses lead shots
my neighbor—repellant

* * *

today on the coastal range a blanket
of Starlings cover our car

a bedsheet of life and lightness
a wonderment of dazed air

the rise and fall—this winged ballet
the gifted grace of a murmuration

a new American acclimation

The God Huitzilopochtli, *Ardea herodias*, the immigrant, is also a dreamer

the last grass harvest done
she can't see her image

in this field, at least for now
maybe she knows the field will green in time

this wait, she stands on eclipsed legs
charmed frills discarded, children left behind,

no messages to deliver,
no gods to please

her slate blue has the tired look of end of year sky,
snake neck hidden on her migrant chest, waiting,

immutable even so far away from her ocean,
so far from other herons just like her

still the Great Blue guards her morsels, drowsy mice
or maybe even few foolish frogs to have, to hold

but how she remembers the taste of fresh fish!
her beak full of song, and in her eyes the dreams of trout

for now, she plants both legs in this cultivated lot
where there's no place to see her own reflection,

she hopes for rewards to come much later,
with fear the curlew will return to claim this valley

Downy Woodpecker and Naked Tree

Dendrócopos pubécens

My leaves have fallen for the last time
while the world awaits to eavesdrop
and learn a way out of these fires
why do they run in circles
to get nowhere fast?

Look! at these unburdened shelf
mushrooms already fat on my bark
and these centipedes that just crawled
last night—at last, a night so clear
that a spider danced on a beam

Sit! place your kindly ear on my lap

Listen! to the echoes left by my Downy
she made nest after nest in my cavity
now I'll keep her chard faint bones
Oh! how I pine for her beak

go!
further down
lower
lower
still
that is the world under this one

Gaze! at my mycelium that gathers
information, unequivocal simple messages
speak of leadership of safety of plenty

Examine! all there is to know
find this path before too long

White-crown Sparrow/Sestina

Zonotríchia leucóphyrys

i fantasize about a White-crown sparrow. She lands softly on my palm
a fat brown scoundrel with prison lines on her head, full of mischief, at play
in and out of hedgerows in groups of twenty, or just one, she creates a current
with her feathers and jumbled whistles—a celebration away from smoke where the bark
is clean and glistening with the moisture of memories of healthy towns where the tie-
strings are between friends—where this bird flies without the fear of fire to break.

This new reality of a world alight in flames, where to gather is dangerous. Maybe we can break
the runaway train of climate change or viruses that plague the very core that palm
obscure, like robbers, slurping the joy of bird song and the child who gathers rope to tie
a noose around the boundless energy of life. Yes. A sparrow to remind us of our play
when smoke, heat, and Gaia were serene. How it was to calmly rest on the smooth bark
of a sycamore, surrounded by family, listening to the sound of rain instead of the current
of bad news and ugly rhetoric. With sparrow in hand, we could preen out of this current
dictating lies broadcasted in contradicting jargon and half-truths. A sparrow to break

this sordid state. Imagine the warmth of her scaly legs, her inquisitive eyes, her beak a bark,
a small song of spring and future with bountiful blessings. A White-crown sparrow on the palm-
tree of childhood. She flies unencumbered in clean skies without a red sun from fires that play
pandemonium and consume acres of trees, flesh, and ambition. Where children no longer tie

long streamers for their kites, where they run with spiraling legs, each leap to tie
the best score in their game. A sparrow in hand could take them, to watch the current
of Pachamama's power, the health of a small blue planet where there is no hesitation of a play on a stage where neighbor can touch a stranger without the need of a mask to break
the power of a smile beneath eyes that clamor affinity. i want this White-crown on the palm
of every child, so she could see a sky free of smog, stars at night, and catch caterpillars on bark

salubrious with her gaiety, prospering forward, driven by the uproarious bark
of her community's encouragement to chase clouds, earth-worms, and wishes that tie
fishing poles, that catch mercury-free fish, slippery, and solvent, but easy to palm
gently, whose scales released into waters rich with the fulfill-ment of dreams and a current
of satisfaction from healing her planet, so that she can raise her own without having to break
in search of a new place to feed her children. A White-crown sparrow her kindred could play

in this hopeful world. Gifted to her from hard work, cooperation, and science at play
with her in mind— not the needs of corporations. Here in this sparrow-world, she sails in a bark
propelled by sails and oars of her own making. Fulfilling her days at peace so that at day's break
she can glory with the White-crown sparrow in her hand, a small reminder that to tie
equal notes of affection and health she needs to plant the seeds that can give a current
of salvation for her children, and her children's children, to hold palm in palm.

Now, imagine this, see her play free in clean soil without pollutants, without the bark
of doomsday at her ankles, enjoying a tie of cool breeze and sunny skies free from the current
that announces the impending break. Instead, she holds a White-crown sparrow in her palm.

xiii

XII

Graylag Goose

Anser anser

Only for the ride
to a castle
I got to be a man
No—
not just a man
a coachman!
for those precious
moments, I thought—
but then, as I preen
my luscious feathers
I'm relieved
to have an orange beak

Acknowledgments

So thankful to Nancy Knowles, Ryan Scariano, Carissa Rose Cummings, and Nick Neely, for their insightful critiques of these poems.

Thanks also to Mary Petiet and Sea Crow Press for giving these poems a place to fly, and Dale Chaplin for the beautiful cover art.

My deepest gratitude to all the editors who have published some earlier forms of these poems, and giving them a place to nest:

Anvil Tongue:
"Towhee"

Willawaw Journal:
"Brewer's or Grackle"
"Mystical Woodpecker"

Amethyst Review-New Writing Engaged in the Sacred:
"Black-Capped Chickadee"
"Clark's Nutcraker"

Eclectica Magazine:
"House Wren"

Verseweavers the Oregon Poetry Association Anthology of Prize-winning Poems:
"White-Crown Sparow/Sestina Poem"

Hare's Paw Review:
"Western Bluebird"

Writers Resist:
"The Wild Turkey is a Good Mother
"Brown-Headed Cowbird."

Center for Humans and Nature's 'Story and Ideas:
"Brown Pelican"
"Downy Woodpecker and Naked Tree"
"Ivory-billed Woodpecker"

The Poeming Pigeon:
"Mourning Dove"

Brown Sugar Zine:
"Wilson's Phalarope"
"Western Gull"

"Sooty Tern" appeared in *Fossils on a Red Flag,*
Finishing Line Press, 2021

Cirque a Literary Journal for the North Pacific Rim, "Double-Crested Cormorant at Tamani Pesh-wa"

About the Author

Amelia Díaz Ettinger is the author of four previous books of poetry: *Self Dissection* (The Poetry Box), *Learning to Love a Western Sky* (Airlie Press), *Speaking at a Time /Hablando a la Vez* (Redbat Press), and *Fossils in a Red Flag* (Finishing Line Press). In an earlier version of herself, Amelia Díaz Ettinger trained as an ornithologist at Washington State University. Her passion for birds has been a constant in her tumulus wandering life. In this work she pays homage to the feather birds that have given her so much solace.

About the Press

Sea Crow Press

Sea Crow Press is an award-winning woman-run independent book publisher based on Cape Cod in Massachusetts committed to amplifying voices that might otherwise go unheard. In a rapidly changing world, we believe the small press plays an essential part in contemporary arts as a community forum, a cultural reservoir, and an agent of change. We are international with a focus on our New England roots. We publish creative nonfiction, fiction, and poetry and our books celebrate our connection to each other and to the natural world with a focus on positive change and great storytelling. We have been building a literary community since 2020.

Author's Note

These Hollowed Bones comprises forty-seven poems written with minimal punctuation. The human voices and most names are without capitalization to indicate the lower standing that humans have within the body of the work, whereas, the persona poems the personal 'I' is capitalized to indicate the higher standing birds have in our milieu.

Printed in the USA
CPSIA information can be obtained
at www.ICGtesting.com
LVHW091814071024
793189LV00033B/491

9 781961 864009